THE NEW YORK GIANTS

BY JOANNE MATTERN

EPIC

BELLWETHER MEDIA ★ MINNEAPOLIS, MN

EPIC BOOKS are no ordinary books. They burst with intense action, high-speed heroics, and shadows of the unknown. Are you ready for an Epic adventure?

This edition first published in 2024 by Bellwether Media, Inc.

Library of Congress Cataloging-in-Publication Data

Names: Mattern, Joanne, 1963- author.
Title: The New York Giants / by Joanne Mattern.
Description: Minneapolis, MN : Bellwether Media, 2024. | Series: Epic. NFL team profiles | Includes bibliographical references and index. | Audience: Ages 7-12 | Audience: Grades 2-3 | Summary: "Engaging images accompany information about the New York Giants. The combination of high-interest subject matter and light text is intended for students in grades 2 through 7"-- Provided by publisher.
Identifiers: LCCN 2023021962 (print) | LCCN 2023021963 (ebook) | ISBN 9798886874891 (library binding) | ISBN 9798886876772 (ebook)
Subjects: LCSH: New York Giants (Football team)--History--Juvenile literature.
Classification: LCC GV956.N4 M357 2024 (print) | LCC GV956.N4 (ebook) | DDC 796.332/64097471--dc23/eng/20230517
LC record available at https://lccn.loc.gov/2023021962
LC ebook record available at https://lccn.loc.gov/2023021963

Editor: Betsy Rathburn Designer: Jeffrey Kollock

Printed in the United States of America, North Mankato, MN.

TABLE OF CONTENTS

HELMET CATCH!

ELI MANNING

The Giants face the Patriots in **Super Bowl** 42. Giants **quarterback** Eli Manning fights off Patriots **defenders**. He throws a long pass to **wide receiver** David Tyree.

Tyree catches the ball against his helmet. This amazing play helps the Giants win the Super Bowl!

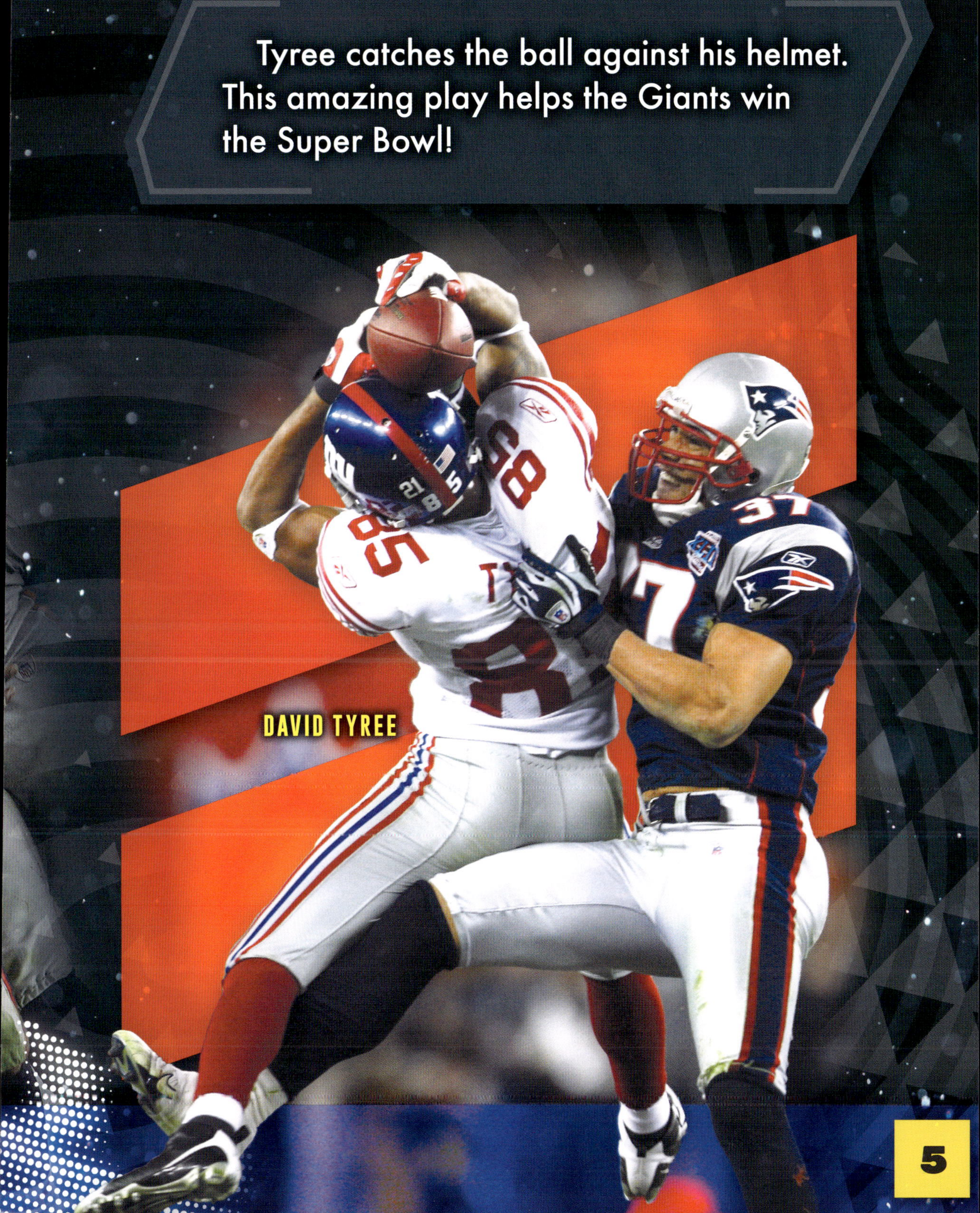

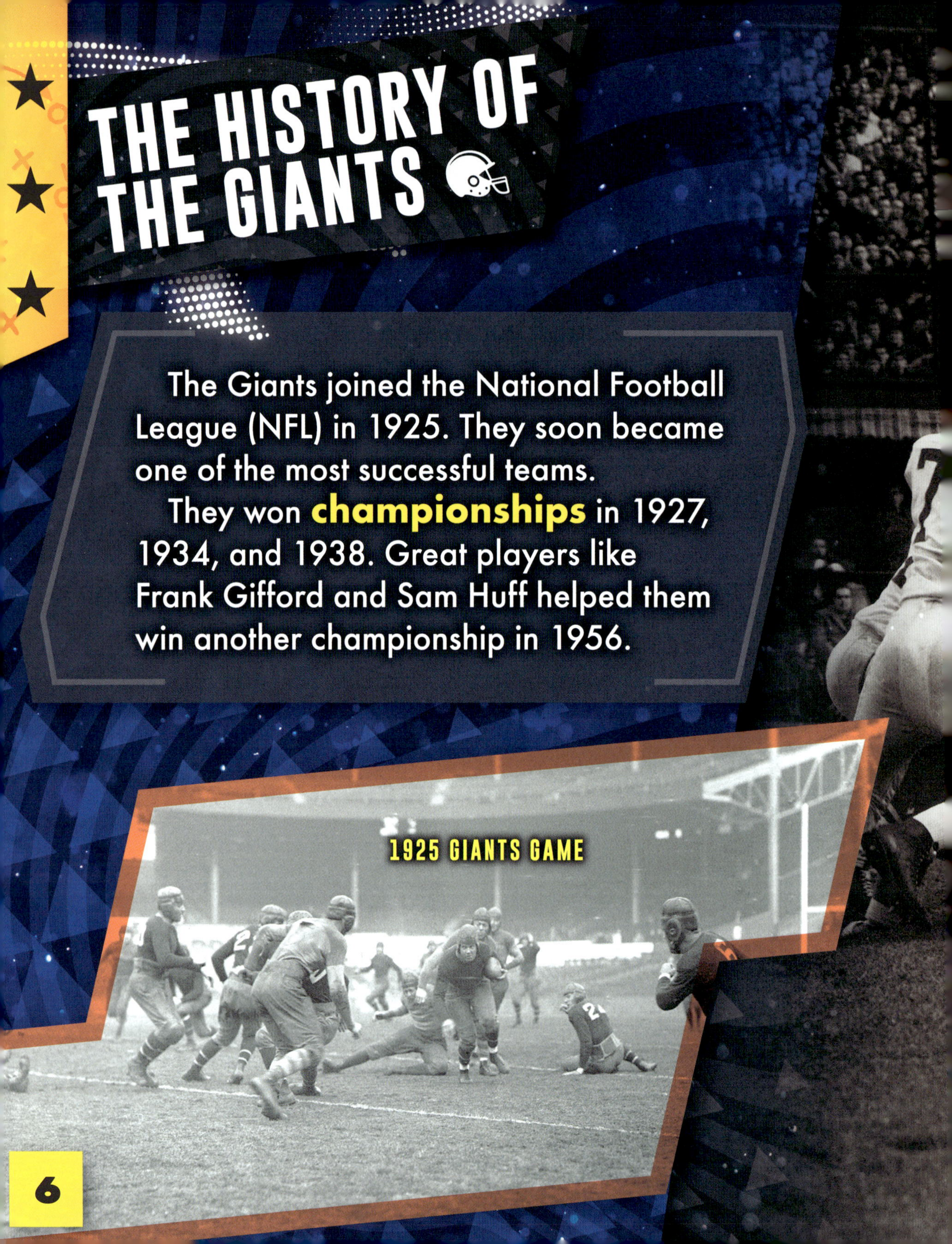

THE HISTORY OF THE GIANTS

The Giants joined the National Football League (NFL) in 1925. They soon became one of the most successful teams.

They won **championships** in 1927, 1934, and 1938. Great players like Frank Gifford and Sam Huff helped them win another championship in 1956.

1925 GIANTS GAME

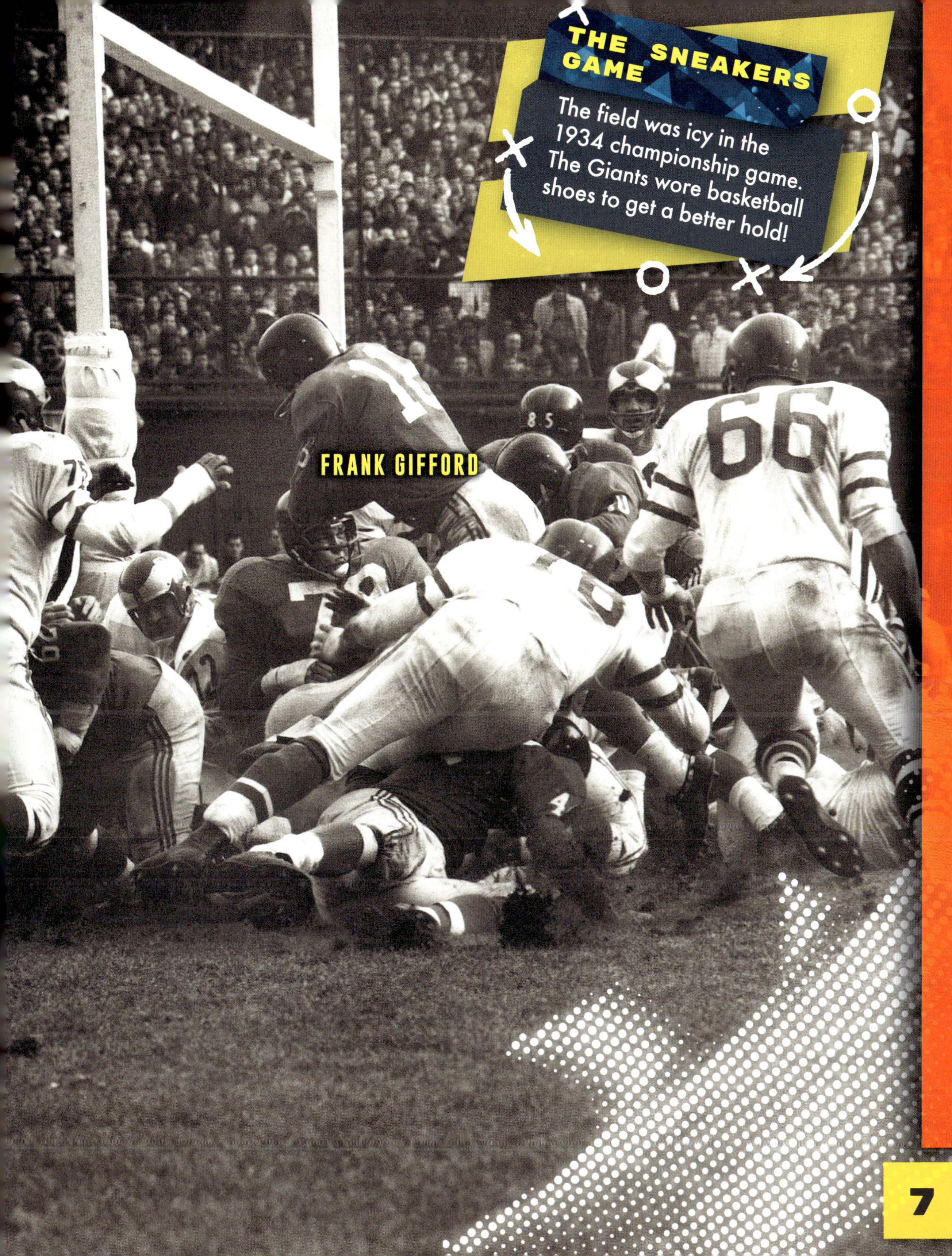

THE SNEAKERS GAME

The field was icy in the 1934 championship game. The Giants wore basketball shoes to get a better hold!

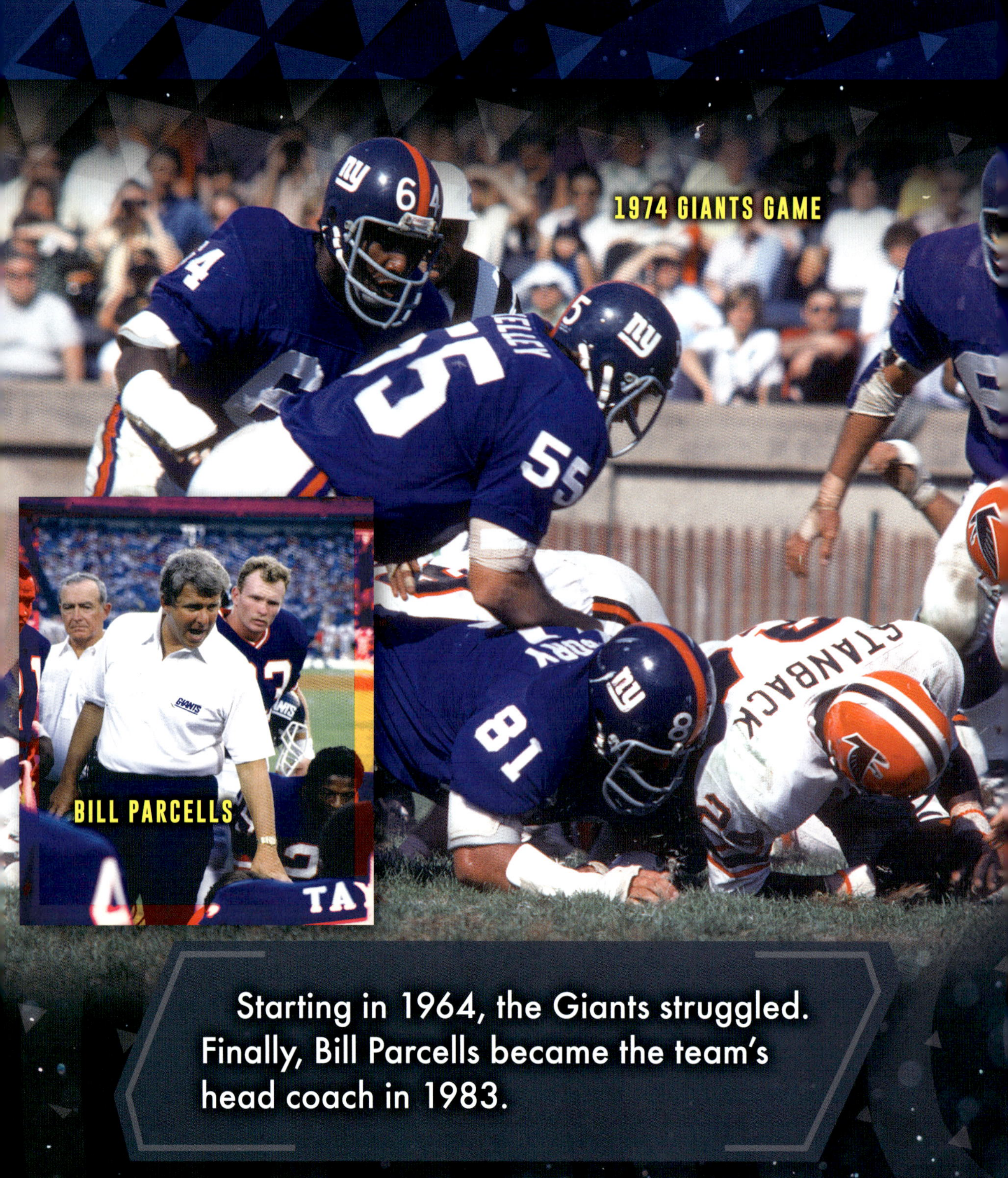

Starting in 1964, the Giants struggled. Finally, Bill Parcells became the team's head coach in 1983.

The Giants got better. They won the Super Bowl in 1987 and 1991. Quarterback Phil Simms and **running back** Ottis Anderson were Super Bowl **MVPs**!

The Giants struggled through the rest of the 1990s. They made the **playoffs** two more times.

1990 GIANTS GAME

In 2001, they played in the Super Bowl again. But they lost the game.

SUPER BOWL 35

In 2004, Eli Manning joined the team. He led the Giants to Super Bowl wins in 2008 and 2012.

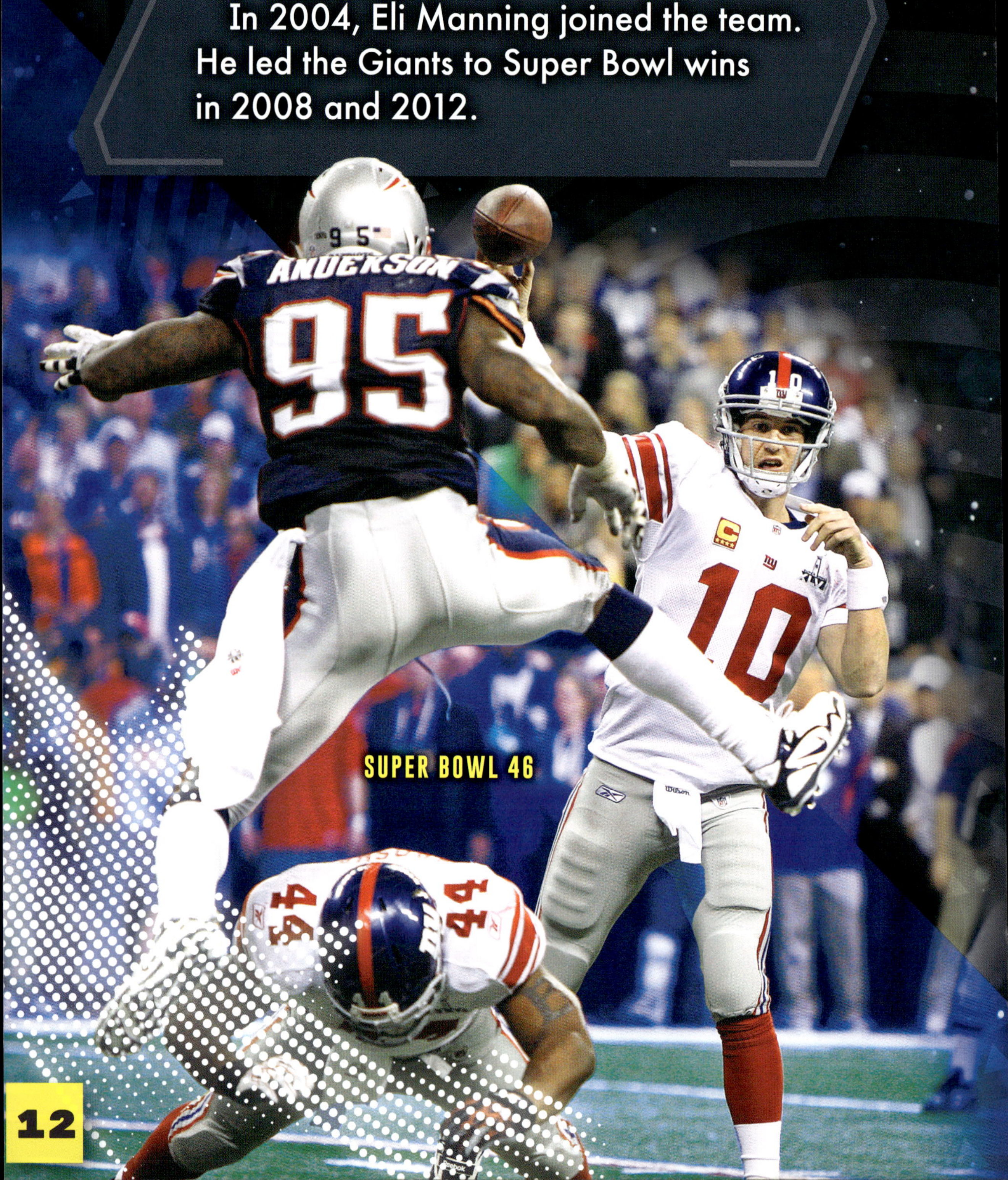

SUPER BOWL 46

Since then, the Giants have rarely made the playoffs. But they hope to win another Super Bowl in the future!

THE GIANTS TODAY

SHARING THE FIELD

The Giants share MetLife Stadium with the New York Jets.

The Giants play in the NFC East. They play at MetLife **Stadium** in East Rutherford, New Jersey.

The Philadelphia Eagles are the Giants' biggest **rival**. They first played in 1933. Their rivalry is over 90 years old!

LOCATION

METLIFE STADIUM

East Rutherford, New Jersey

NEW JERSEY

N
W E
S

GAME DAY!

Before home games, Giants fans gather for fun at MetLife Stadium. They play games and show off their football skills.

Inside the stadium, the stands are filled with blue, red, and white. Fans yell and cheer for their team!

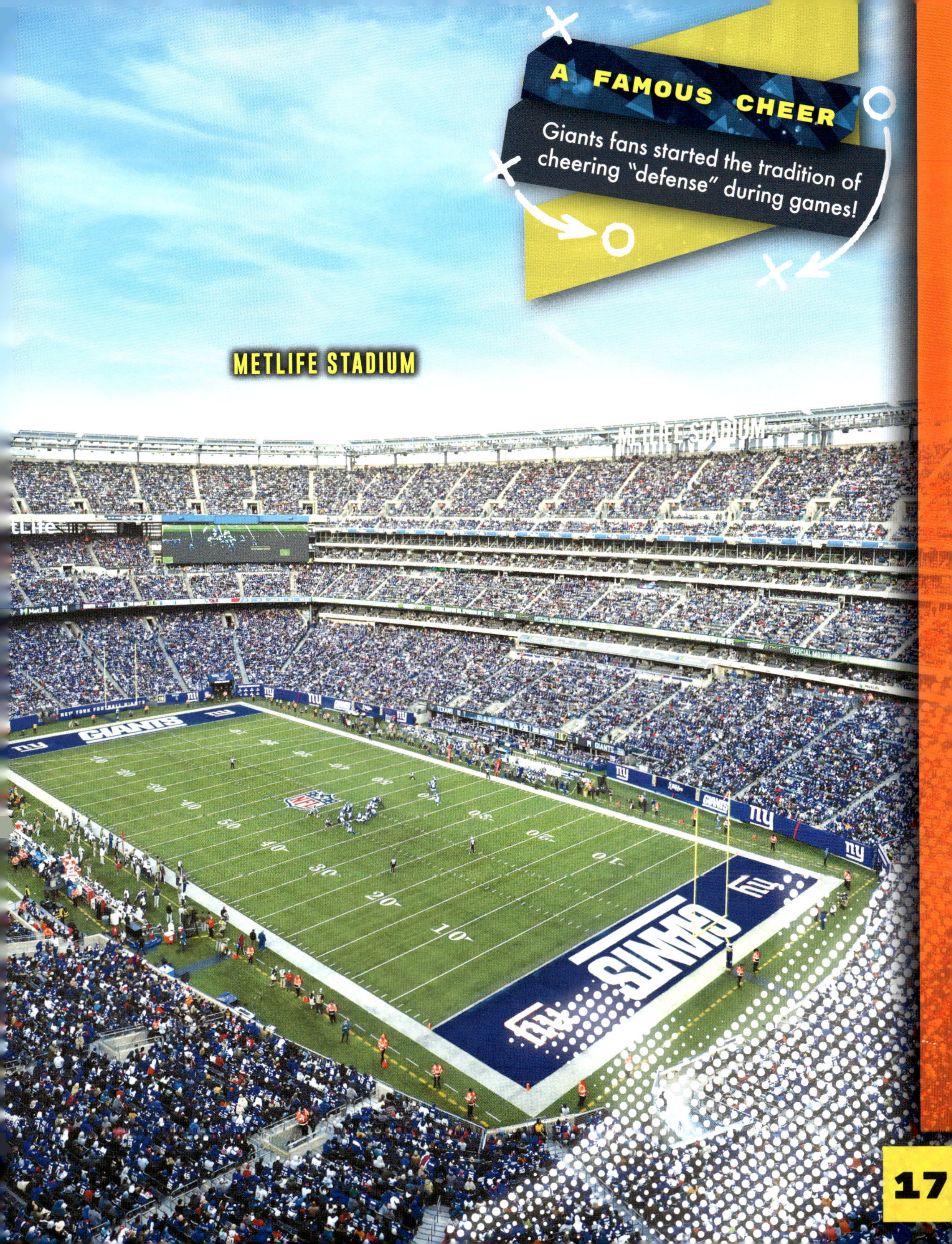

A FAMOUS CHEER

Giants fans started the tradition of cheering "defense" during games!

METLIFE STADIUM

The Giants helped start a favorite football **tradition**. After a big win in 1984, players poured Gatorade on Coach Parcells.

Now, teams often pour Gatorade on coaches after wins. Giants fans love to see their team win!

GATORADE POUR IN 2022

★ FAMOUS PLAYERS ★

MEL HEIN
Center
Played 1931–1945

OTTIS ANDERSON
Running Back
Played 1986–1992

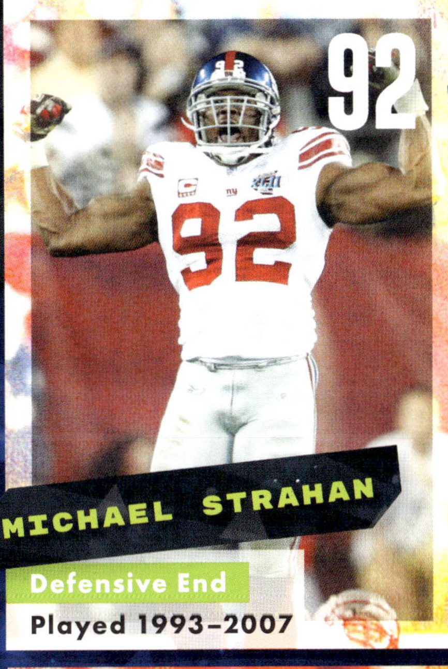

MICHAEL STRAHAN
Defensive End
Played 1993–2007

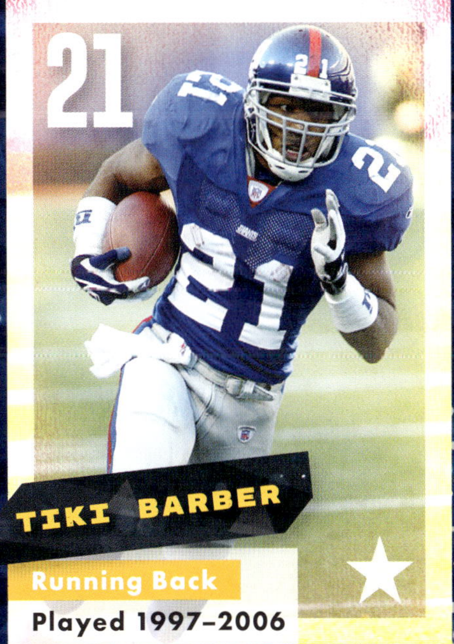

TIKI BARBER
Running Back
Played 1997–2006

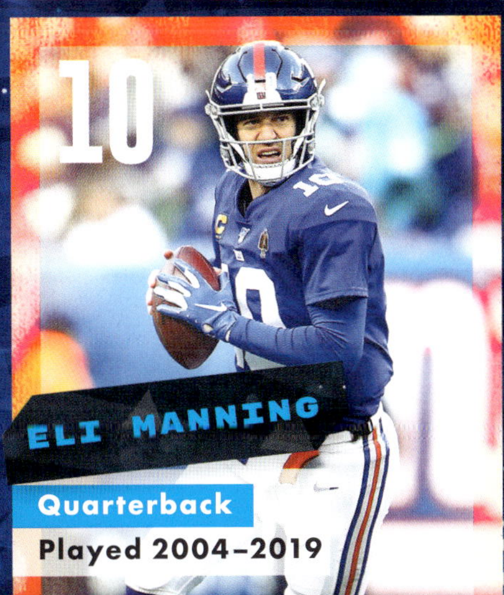

ELI MANNING
Quarterback
Played 2004–2019

NEW YORK GIANTS FACTS

LOGO

JOINED THE NFL | 1925

NICKNAME | Big Blue

MASCOT

NONE

CONFERENCE

National Football Conference (NFC)

COLORS

DIVISION | NFC East

Dallas Cowboys

Philadelphia Eagles

Washington Commanders

STADIUM

★ METLIFE STADIUM ★

opened April 10, 2010

holds 82,500 people

TIMELINE

1925
The Giants play their first season

1927
The Giants win their first championship

1983
Bill Parcells becomes the Giants' head coach

1987
The Giants win their first Super Bowl

2012
The Giants win their fourth Super Bowl

★ RECORDS ★

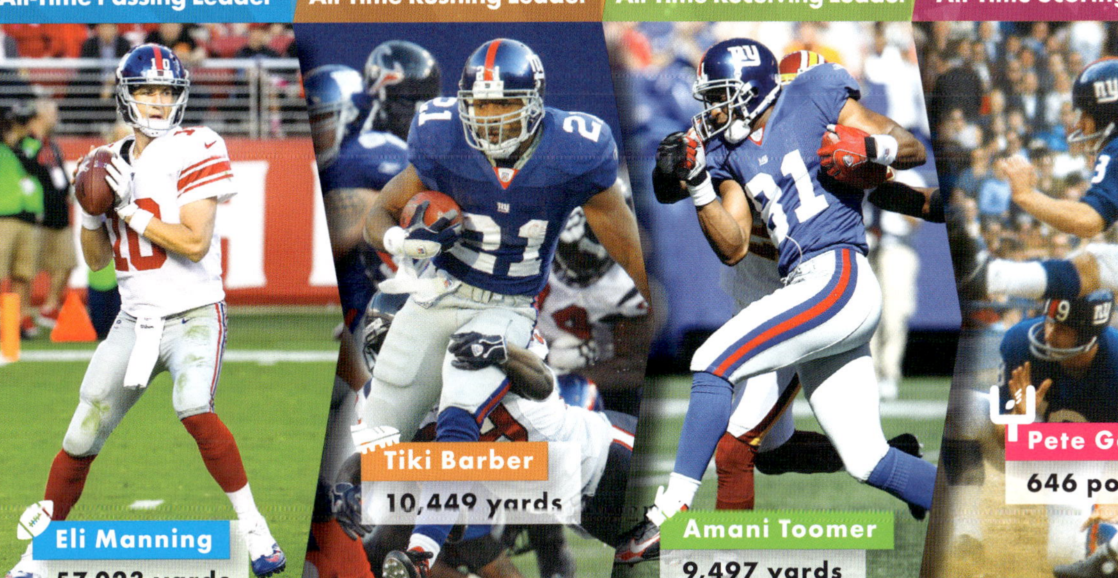

All-Time Passing Leader	All-Time Rushing Leader	All-Time Receiving Leader	All-Time Scoring Leader
Eli Manning	Tiki Barber	Amani Toomer	Pete Gogolak
57,023 yards	10,449 yards	9,497 yards	646 points

GLOSSARY

championships—contests to decide the best team or person

defenders—players who try to stop the opposing team from scoring

MVPs—most valuable players; MVPs are players who contribute the most to their team's success

playoffs—games played after the regular season is over; playoff games determine which teams play in the championship game.

quarterback—a player whose main job is to throw and hand off the ball

rival—a long-standing opponent

running back—a player whose main job is to run with the ball

stadium—an arena where sports are played

Super Bowl—the annual championship game of the NFL

tradition—a special way people celebrate or honor something

wide receiver—a player whose main job is to catch passes from the quarterback

TO LEARN MORE

AT THE LIBRARY

Abdo, Kenny. *New York Giants.* Minneapolis, Minn.: Abdo Zoom, 2022.

Hill, Christina. *Inside the New York Giants.* Minneapolis, Minn.: Lerner Publications, 2023.

Myers, Carrie. *Eagles vs. Giants.* Minnetonka, Minn.: Kaleidoscope Pub., 2019.

ON THE WEB

FACTSURFER

Factsurfer.com gives you a safe, fun way to find more information.

1. Go to www.factsurfer.com.
2. Enter "New York Giants" into the search box and click 🔍.
3. Select your book cover to see a list of related content.

INDEX

The images in this book are reproduced through the courtesy of: ASSOCIATED PRESS/ AP Images, front cover, p. 21 (1927); Felix Mizioznikov, front cover, p. 15; Mitchell Leff/ Getty Images, pp. 3, 23; MediaNews Group/ Boston Herald/ Getty Images, p. 4; New York Daily News Archive/ Getty Images, p. 5; Bettmann/ Getty Images, pp. 6, 21 (1925); Robert Riger/ Getty Images, pp. 6-7; Focus On Sport/ Getty Images, pp. 8-9, 19 (Ottis Anderson), 21 (1983, 1987), 21 (Pete Gogolak); Sporting News Archive/ Getty Images, p. 9; Al GOLUB/ AP Images, p. 10; Kevin Reece/ AP Images, p. 11; Boston Globe/ Getty Images, pp. 12-13; Jim McIsaac/ Getty Images, p. 14; NFL/ Wikipedia, pp. 15 (logo), 20 (logos); Alex Trautwig/ Getty Images, p. 16; Adam Hunger/ AP Images, pp. 16-17; Evan Pinkus/ AP Images, pp. 18-19; JOHN LINDSAY/ AP Images, p. 19 (Mel Hein); REUTERS/ Alamy, pp. 19 (Michael Strahan), 21 (Tiki Barber); JOHN ANGELILLO/ Alamy, p. 19 (Tiki Barber), 21 (Amani Toomer); Mike Stobe/ Getty Images, p. 19 (Eli Manning); Vincent Alban/ Getty Images, p. 20 (mascot); Gabe Shakour, p. 20 (stadium); Tom Hauck/ Alamy, p. 21 (2012); Cal Sport Media/ Alamy, p. 21 (Eli Manning).